# THE
# FIGHT
# FOR YOUR
# LIFE

CHRISTOPHER M. BONNER

ISBN: 979-8-88640-544-6 (sc)
ISBN: 979-8-88640-545-3 (hc)
ISBN: 979-8-88640-546-0 (e)

Because of the dynamic nature of the Internet, any web addresses or links contained in this book may have changed since publication and may no longer be valid. The views expressed in this work are solely those of the author and do not necessarily reflect the views of the publisher, and the publisher hereby disclaims any responsibility for them.

THE EWINGS PUBLISHING

One Galleria Blvd., Suite 1900, Metairie, LA 70001
1-888-421-2397

# CONTENTS

# FOREWORD

..................................................................................................

**A**s it relates to God there is no gray area. The scriptures even say that you're either for Him or against Him. There is no middle ground or straddling the fence. If you are not for God, then that means you are fight against Him. What you are fight for is control of your life. You are trying to control your life, while God is also seeking control of your life. He wants to govern your life according to His plan and purpose for you, which leads to abundant life, peace, and prosperity. On the other hand, you want to control your life, so you can live without discipline to be frivolous and careless until your life spirals out of control.

I know it sounds old-fashioned, but we still need the hand of God to guide us through life. Even more-so now that we are seeing scripture fulfilled in life. People are turning away from sound doctrine and want to hear something that entertains them or makes them feel good. Church congregations are becoming diminished because people would rather watch church services from their phones or at home on their computers. It's great that they are still hearing great preaching by watching livestreams, but they are missing the fellowship or personal interaction with other believers. This is the essence of the kingdom of God. There must be interaction. The kingdom of God cannot not grow without personal interaction of the believers. The believers cannot spiritually multiply and replenish without personal interaction. This is just like having children. A husband and wife cannot conceive a child without personal interaction. Likewise, is the Kingdom of God.

With so many people abstaining from fellowship and worship, it leads to fighting with God. Because you are not seeking to connect with God, you are being distracted by all the influences discussed in this book. Being overcome by these influences puts you at odds with God. Because you are fighting with God, it is obviously you who suffer from it. When you could have a life that is flourishing with your heart's desire, you are instead stressing yourself out every day by trying to do things your way. Hopefully by the end of this book you will know where you stand with God. If you are in contention with Him, then take the step of faith and throw in the towel. Surrender to Him and let Him the Lord of your life.

# CHAPTER ONE

# THE FIGHT

I n this life, everyone who has a relationship with God, wants it to be a healthy and wholesome one. However, as you go through life and deal with all the issues that life brings, you oftentimes find yourself at odds with God. I know this sounds strange and unusual for the Christian because typically when you think of someone being at odds with or fighting with God, it is usually those who do not have a relationship with him. On the contrary, everyone, whether you have a personal relationship with God or not, is fighting with God, or has fought with God. The question becomes; do those with the personal relationship have a greater fight or do those without? You could debate and belabor this point for eternity. Yet, I do not think there is definite answer. The reason is because God loves you. Whether you accept His love or not, does not change His love for you. It is this love that causes one to fight. Ironically, the fight of your life, is the fight for your life. He is fighting to draw you unto Himself and you are fighting to have your own way. Believe it or not, He is fighting to give you the best of life. However, because you are blinded by the world's system, you think you can achieve the best of life on your own.

The greatest example of the fight between God and Man was demonstrated by Jesus in the garden of Gethsemane. According to the book of Matthew chapter 26, It was here that Jesus showed the fullness of his humanity, while being fully aware in his divinity. This gave Him full knowledge that He would lose the fight with God. He pleaded with God to let the cup pass from Him. This means He desired of God to not let Him go through His Cross experience. Again, in Jesus' humanity, He knew the agony he would suffer in being crucified on the cross. The sheer pain he would feel, the trauma of asphyxiation while struggling to breath. He knew the terror of the full experience up to the point of breathing the last breath and dying. Because of this, Jesus expressed deep disdain with following through with this mission. Nevertheless, despite the horror of it all, He knew it was God's will for Him and the fulfillment of the purpose for which He came to earth. So, while in the fullness of his human nature, He urged God with everything in him, to change his destiny. Though, knowing fully in his divine nature, that he must go through the cross, lest the world be lost. And in moving strongly in faith and obedience to the Father's Will, Jesus obligingly conceded and declared the infamous words of a true Christian, "Nevertheless, not my will but yours be done".

This is the fight of your life. It is the fight to carry out your own will instead of surrendering to the will of God The Father. It would be wise to concede and surrender like Jesus did, but unfortunately, it is not that easy for you and me. It is difficult for you and me because you and I are obviously not divinity wrapped in humanity, like Jesus was. When Jesus was born, he was imparted into Mary by the Holy Spirit. So, in other words, he was God in the flesh. He came down from heaven as God and took on a human flesh that He could be an example to us in the earth. You and I, however, were born of flesh and in flesh. We had to go through life trying to feel and find our way until such time that we come into the knowledge of God and accept Jesus as our savior. You might think that once you reach this point of accepting the savior, then you fully surrender to God and you live in blissful peace and harmony with Him. This could not be farther from reality. What you must realize is that accepting Jesus Christ as Savior, is simply the first step of your renewed life that you know to be salvation. However, there is a critical second stage that comes after, which is transformation. Some may call it deliverance. You see, in the salvation stage, this is a work of the heart. The heart, spiritually speaking, is the nature of a person. It is your core being. It is what makes you who you are. So, with salvation, you have an awareness in the core of your being that you need God to live life prosperously, successfully, and most of all Holy!

Obviously, if one has not accepted salvation, there is a fight between you and God to accept him and surrender your will to His. God is fighting that you may have life more abundantly as promised by Jesus in the book of John chapter 10. While it may sound old fashioned and outdated, the true alternative to not accepting Jesus and salvation is to live eternity in damnation and torment. Because of the love God has for you, and how He treasures you as His prized creation, He does not want this to be your fate. This is the reason God sent Jesus to us and provided a way for us to escape the penalty of sin and live eternity with Him. This is beautifully described in the book of Romans.

> *Romans 10:9-10(ESV) "If you will confess with your mouth that Jesus is Lord and believe in your heart that God raised him from the dead, you shall be saved. For with the heart one believes and is justified, and with the mouth one confesses and is saved."*

When accepting salvation, you have a change of heart and decide to allow Jesus to come in as Lord and take control of your life. In doing so, He begins working on you to bring about transformation. Having a change of heart is somewhat the easy part. But it is changing your behavior that is the challenge. Having a change of heart, is actually realizing that you need to live a better life and accepting Jesus' help to do it. Yet, making the change is a fight. Sometimes it is a life-long battle.

In the transformation stage, it goes beyond the heart and you realize you have to be renewed. The renewal takes place in your mind.

*Romans 12:2 (ESV) "I appeal to you therefore, brothers, by the mercies of God, to present your bodies as a living sacrifice, holy and acceptable to God, which is your spiritual worship. Do not be conformed to this world, but be transformed by the renewal of your mind, that by testing you may discern what is the will of God, what is good and acceptable and perfect."*

In this verse, you are challenged to be a living sacrifice unto God. Does this sound familiar? Doesn't this sound like what God the Father was requiring Jesus to do in the garden of Gethsamane? It is exactly what the Father was requiring of Jesus. You must know that you and I are no different. We have the same requirement of God to be totally surrendered to Him that we may express His Will. The Apostle Paul, who is the writer of the text, even goes as far as to say that being a living sacrifice is your "spiritual worship". Some translations say "your reasonable service". Meaning, if you truly worship God, then everything is completely and fully about Him and not about you. This is not meant to be unfair and one-sided. But it is to say that God knows more about you and what is best for you than you do. The most fascinating part of this scripture is his saying "do not be conformed to this world, but be transformed by renewing your mind". This is where the fight is. It is in your mind. To be transformed you must change your thinking. You can no longer see things as you are used to. You must begin to see things as God sees them. I often tell people, when you change your mind, you change your life. When you think differently, you act differently. The challenge of renewal and transformation is to break the cycles and patterns that you are used to according to the world's system or life as you know it. But instead, you must train yourself to God's system by obedience to His word and yielding to the power of the Holy Spirit.

Finally, in this scripture in Romans 12, you must take notice that there is testing that you undergo to discern the will of God, from the way of the world. Transformation does not just happen, but you must go through tests in order to choose. God allows everyone to have free will. He does not force anyone to change but allows opportunity to choose the right way. Tests come in your life, so that you are given an opportunity to choose the will of God over the way of the world. The way of the world is what appeals to the "good" or natural feeling of our fleshly desires. On the other hand, the will of God, is what you know, deep within, is what's right and best for you. It is what you know pleases God and builds your character to be more like Christ and an example to others. This is difficult and takes a lot of effort. But it is what you were created to do, and in the long run, gives you the most peace with God, joy, and success in life.

Everyone goes through tests, and everyone is not tested according to the same manner. Your particular test is related to your personal desires and needs. Therefore, the tests that you face may not necessarily be the test that someone else faces. Their test may involve lying or infidelity, where your test may deal with anger or bitterness. It is obviously the enemy or evil one who tests you with these issues of your fleshly nature and he wants you to fail and remain in your issue. However, it is God who wants you to overcome the issues and conform to what pleases Him and ultimately makes you better. During this testing period, there is this constant battle going on within you. The Apostle Paul also describes this battle, as he dealt with tests of his own.

> *Romans 7:21(ESV) "So I find it to be a law that when I want to do right, evil lies close at hand. For I delight in the law of God, in my inner being, but I see in my members another law waging war against the law of my mind and making me captive to the law of sin that dwells in my members."*

This explanation from the Apostle is the epitome of fighting with God. Paul recognizes what is right by God and has it in him to do it. But right next to doing right, within him, is the desire to do evil. This is the same fight you and I wage every day. You know when you are in line at the bank teller or the grocery store and the person behind the counter gives you too much money back. Part of you wants to keep the money and act like nothing happened. While the other half of you knows you have to tell the person what happened and give back the excess. You know when you are driving down the street and the car in the next lane switches over in front of you with no signal or warning. There is a part of you that wants to shout expletives and give hand gestures. However, you realize the right thing to do is take a deep breath, say to yourself the person is just in a hurry, and forgive them.

It would be great if situations like this was a one-time experience. Truth is, we face dilemmas of this nature all day every day. It is a daily battle to choose good over evil. While God does not expect us to be perfect and get it right all the time, there is a requirement from Him that we grow daily and get better as life goes on. This is why he showers us with grace. As you read on in Romans chapter 7, you will see how Paul asked God to remove the "thorn" or the test. But God refuses to remove it and declares to Paul that while he often fails the test, he can lean on the grace of God to continue on life's journey.

The grace of God is vitally importantly because, again, you will never be perfect and always make the right decision every time. But God, does not want you to give up and abandon the quest for righteousness altogether. So, God gives grace to let you know that He believes in you and is patient with you while you continue trying. God's grace works the same as the "Grace Period" you are given by your creditors. Each month, at the due date of your payment, there is usually ten additional days tacked on after the due date. These ten days are your grace period. This means your payment is due on the due date but is not deemed late until after the grace period. God sees you the same way. You are expected to get it right on your test, but God does not deem you unrighteous or unworthy unless you fall completely from grace.

While God's grace is a wonderful gift from Him, it is not to be abused. I pray you are not one who has fallen into this habit and are taking God's grace for granted. Have you greatly minimized or totally stopped trying to live righteous? Have you begun to do what I call premeditated sin? This is where you live frivolously and carelessly because you think you can just ask for forgiveness, God's grace will cover you, and everything will be fine. But this is not God's will.

> *Romans 6:1-2 (ESV) "What shall we say then? Are we to continue in sin that grace may abound? By no means! How can we who died to sin still live in it?*

This scripture requires no explanation. It is straight forward and means exactly what is says. To the heart of God, it is betrayal. How can you commit to God then turn your back on him to return to your sinful ways? So, God continues to show you mercy until He sees that you were not serious in your original commitment. At that point, God still does not discontinue His mercy, but He allows the consequences of your actions set in on you. He allows you to feel the affects of your disobedience and unrighteousness, while his grace preserves your life, similar to how he was with JOB. We know in Job's life, he became self-righteous, almost to the point where he thought he deserved preferential treatment from God. To show him the error of his ways, God allowed the devil to put Job through rigorous tests of loss and even sickness. All the while, He preserved his life so he could gain awareness of his faults. You might be living a Job experience right now. You are going through trial after trial. You are suffering loss of possessions, home in foreclosure, even have sickness in your body. All of this is going on with you and you refuse to acknowledge that it is due to your fight with God. You are coming up with many reasons, excuses and people to blame, but the real reason is you are not in good fellowship with God and He is trying hard to get your attention. Just as with Job, friends try to tell you of your wrong, there are many signs, but nothing will work until you come personally to God and allow Him to bring your wrong to your attention.

Understanding that your fight with God is just the beginning. Understanding why you fight is what is important. You must understand the why before you can correct the issue and get your life on track with God. As you continue reading, you will see the various reasons why you fight with God and hopefully understand how to fix it and get in right standing with God to receiving the blessings of life.

## Personal Testimonial

It took me a long time to realize that I was fighting with God. When I was in my late teens and early twenties, I was going through deep depression because I did not like how my life was. Worse than that, I did not know how I was going to change it to make it better. I did not see myself going to college. I did not see myself having the opportunities that others had. I did not see myself having a wife and kids. I thought I was not good enough to really make anything of my life. All these negative thoughts that clouded my mind was just evidence of my fight with God. As you can see, all these thoughts were conjured by me and what I thought of myself. This is where the problem begins. I did not know God and therefore did not know what He thought of me. His thoughts about me were much different than what I thought of myself. This is how I was fighting with Him. His thoughts and plans for me were much greater than what I had for myself.

It was not until I came to know God and surrendered my life fully to Him, that my future got brighter. I began to see doors open. I saw opportunities become available to me. I got a college education. I started seeing blessings in my relationships. I gained new friends who were resources to enhance my life. I met my wife and we began a wonderful life and family together with two great kids. Career opportunities began to open up for me and I was able to make a comfortable living. All this happened when I stopped fighting with God for control of my life. When I turned it over to Him, everything fell into place. I no longer had to fight for what I wanted, but as I walked the path He laid out for me, it all became readily available for me.

It sounds strange, but I learned the less I fought, the easier life became. The more I tried to do it on my own, the more difficult. But when I stopped fighting to make things happen, God graciously put them in my hands. The familiar saying is so true. All we have to do is "Let go and let God have His way".

## The Challenge

1.  Evaluate your life to see if everything is how you want it.

2.  Ask yourself if you have the greater control or does God.

3.  If you do not have a personal relationship with God, begin praying and asking Him to reveal Himself to you.

4.  Pray and ask God to help you yield to your faith and trust Him to guide you.

5.  Totally surrender to God. Let go and let Him have His way in your life.

# CHAPTER TWO

# DISBELIEF

**B**elief or believing in something is the most fundamental element, not just in the Christian life, but in life period. Everything about your life is based on belief. You can look at it from the most essential or the most medial standpoint and still draw the same conclusion. For instance, for you to sit in a chair there is a subliminal belief that the chair is going to support you and not crumble under you. Likewise, when you lie down to sleep each night, you have a belief that the bed is not going to break down when you crawl up in it. To understand this at a greater level, each time you lie down at night, there is the belief that you will awake the next morning to care for the things required in that day. The reason I know this is because many people develop a schedule and make plans each night before bed for what they must do the next day. If there was not a belief that you would awake the next day, there would be no reason to make plans for what you will do.

Believing is a vital part of life. Your entire life is established on what you believe. You believe you are going to get the job. Therefore, you submit your resume and fill out the application. You believe that person will go out with you. That is why you approach them and strike up a conversation. You believe you are going to score well on the test. For that reason, you stay up late studying. You believe the doctor can help to heal you or make you feel better. Therefore, you make an appointment for an office visit. You believe that you will make the team. That is why you rush to the gym after school to get in the try-outs. You have a belief that you can swim and will not drown. This belief leads you to fearlessly jump into the pool. Life has no direction without believing in something or someone. You feel lost or misguided without someone or something to believe in. Belief establishes foundation and stability for life. Without it we have no basis to build our lives and move from one stage of life to the next.

Obviously if belief is this important to the general things of life, like sitting in a chair or simply believing in a bed to support you while you sleep, then how critical do you think belief is when you add in the God-Factor. True, you can have belief in many things in life and not factor in God's influence. However, if you do this you have just started the fight with God. Reason is if you go though life and not factor in the fact that God is in total control, then that is a definite sign of disbelief. Disbelief in God creates a terrible rift between you and Him. You might even look at is as an extreme case of tug-of-war. God is pulling you toward faith in Him to guide and direct your path, while you are pulling away from God to try and establish your own way. As I mentioned in chapter one, God already has an established plan for your life and the more you fight against Him, the more difficult you make your life. When you do not believe in God, or believe God, then you are fighting against Him for what is best in your life. The reason I distinguished the two scenarios of believing God and believing in God, is because there is a vast difference between the two. Yet, both are evidence of fighting with God. Not believing in God is the lesser of the two fights, because you are disavowing God completely. You are in essence, saying that God does not exist. You are saying that there is no God. Many have tried to prove this time and time again. Each time they come up with inconclusive evidence. This lack of evidence is proof enough that God is real. And with that said, just because someone does not believe in God, that does not negate the fact that God still is active in that person's life. As a matter of fact, you who believe, lived for a time when you did not. Even during that time, God was still present in your life. If for no other reason, He was there sustaining your life. After all, He is the only one who controls life and death. During that scary time in your life when you thought you would not make, it was God who would not let death have victory over your life. This is the evidence of God's grace, mercy and favor. For even when you do not believe in Him, His love still prevails and causes Him to move on your behalf. While God's goodness is awesome, your disbelief in Him or your fight with Him, is not without consequence. Because you do not believe in God, but still benefit from His goodness, you still have dire consequences that result from your fight with God. Everything you try is a struggle and very few things are ever accomplished. Those things that you do accomplish do not last long because you are without God's power to sustain them. So you constantly fight through life, only to get to the end being extremely exhausted and unfulfilled.

Not believing God is the greater of the two fights of disbelief. Not believing God is greater than not believing in God because it makes no sense to believe in God, but not believe what He says. I must admit, I am very scared for people who say they believe in God, yet do not believe the plan He has for their lives. It is almost like you are dying of thirst and someone you know and trust, tells you for sure there is a body of water over the hill. But for whatever reason, you will not believe them to go and get a drink and you end up perishing for disbelief. You make your own life extremely hard because you fight with God over believing what His word says for your life. You can believe that God is real, but not real enough to believe His word or what He has for your life. You would rather fight with God as He tries to lead you in a life of blessing and peace, than to believe Him and embrace the blessings and peace.

God wants to make your marriage better, but you fight Him.

He wants to bless your children and help you be a parent or better parent, but you fight Him.

He wants to move you from job to career, but you fight Him.

He wants to help you open the business, but you fight Him.

He wants to help you write the book, but you fight Him.

He wants to help you finish or go back to school, but you fight Him.

He wants to help you fix your financial problems, but you fight Him.

He wants to help you build or strengthen your ministry, but you fight Him.

He wants to improve your health, but you fight Him.

God has all of these blessings in store for you, but you block them all because you choose to fight God by not believing Him to do it for you. When you live in disbelief, you hinder every blessing that God has in store for you. You would rather struggle to try and do it on your own, than to believe God and do it His way.

You must know that when you are in the fight with God, you are not always on the offensive. It is not always that you are throwing punches of disbelief at God, while he tries to block them with His shield of grace and mercy. There are times when God is on the offensive and you are on the defensive.

> *Hebrews 11:6 (ESV) "And without faith it is impossible to please him, for whoever would draw near to God must believe that he exists and that he rewards those who seek him"*

When God gets fed up with your punching Him with disbelief, He oftentimes puts you in the ropes and delivers a series of "withholding" jabs. By this I mean, God withholds the rewards of good and perfect gifts from those who do not seek Him by faith. Your belief leads you to faith in

God that pushes you to carry out what He directs you to in your life. Since there is no belief, you have no faith to bring forth what God promised. Obviously, according to the scripture, this displeases God. When God is displeased, He forces you into the ropes of destitution and stings you with jab after jab of withholding blessings. This hurts severely because you have expectations of what you want and desire, yet you are lacking the faith to please God, which would cause Him to manifest it. Instead, you suffer the pain of missing out on the gift of God.

God is the only one I know who can hurt you the most just by distancing Himself. By withholding the things you need, God is delivering the most powerful blows that life can dish out. With your disbelief and lack of effort to seek God, you force Him to retaliate by remaining at a distance in your life and watching you suffer through one poor decision after another. Without a doubt, it hurts Him as much as it does you, but He has no choice. He has to follow the plan you set, since you will not follow His.

So disbelief is extremely detrimental to your life and the worst fight you can have with God. One of the most profound examples of disbelief in the bible is when Jesus was restricted from performing miracles for His own people. This came right after He had left a foreign land where He performed many miracles.

> *Matthew 13:53-58 (NKJV) "Now it came to pass, when Jesus had finished these parables, that He departed from there. [54] When He had come to His own country, He taught them in their synagogue, so that they were astonished and said, "Where did this Man get this wisdom and these mighty works? [55] Is this not the carpenter's son? Is not His mother called Mary? And His brothers James, Joses, Simon, and Judas? [56] And His sisters, are they not all with us? Where then did this Man get all these things?" [57] So they were offended at Him.*

*But Jesus said to them, "A prophet is not without honor except in his own country and in his own house." [58] Now He did not do many mighty works there because of their unbelief."*

This scripture is a prime example of how one can hurt God the most. When his own will not receive His Son and honor His Son, this is the greatest blow that can be dealt to God. Obviously, Jesus was extremely hurt because He no doubt, wanted to perform miracles for His own people. This was especially true since He had just arrived from a foreign land where He was able to perform many miracles for them. However, when He came to His own hometown, His own did not receive Him as the Messiah. They did not recognize Him as the Son of God. Instead, they downgraded Him to being just a simple carpenter's son. Just a simple man, with an average family like the rest. And with His display of wisdom He taught, they thought He had no right and were offended by His actions. Wow, what a fight. With His desire to work miracles for them, and their extreme disbelief, this was a fight of epic proportion.

It is easy to look at this story and shake our heads in disdain for how Jesus' own people acted toward Him. But how does it feel to know that you and I have or are just as guilty right now. God is working through Jesus to perform miracles in your life as well. But, because your belief is not at the level of where it needs to be, He is unable to work on your behalf.

You could be needing Him to heal a loved one, like the father in the book of Mark chapter 9. The father had a son who was mentally ill and wanted Jesus to heal him. Jesus asked the father do you believe, for all things are possible to the one who believes. The father's reply was priceless. He said I do believe. But help my unbelief. Can you admit, like the father, that you have unbelief and it is hindering God from working a miracle in your life? All you have to do is surrender your disbelief to God as the father did on behalf of his son. If you do this regarding your situation, God can deal with your disbelief and work on your behalf just as he did with this father.

It is not uncommon to find yourself in situations that seem too hard for God. Typically, what happens, is the tragedies of life are so overwhelming that it seems there is no way out. It seems there is no positive way for it to end. Because of what you are familiar with from past experiences or with what happened to someone else, you think your results will be the same. I must tell you that this is exactly what the enemy wants you to think. Satan wants your mind to be cluttered with doubt and filled with disbelief in God. But I want to encourage you to have faith and never doubt. Trust in the word and power of God to turn your situation around for your good. The scripture is so very true. All things are possible to everyone who believes. Stop fighting with God through disbelief. Surrender to His will and allow Him to do a new thing, a great thing, in your life.

## Personal Testimonial

Even after I totally surrendered my life to God, it took me a while to gain strong faith to overcome all my disbeliefs. I can admit that it is overwhelming and uncomfortable stepping into your calling and place of purpose when you are new in your faith. To see yourself doing things that you never thought possible and express yourself with an anointing that you never recognized, gives you a feeling of mystery. My greatest challenge of disbelief came when God began moving me into my calling as a minister and pastor. This was never on my list of "things-to-do". I never really imagined myself being a preacher. For the bulk of my life, I have been shy and never liked being the center of attention. On top of all that, I never thought I knew enough about the bible and God to preach or teach it to anyone. I knew how to navigate and understand it well enough to get through the personal things of my life. But teaching it to someone else did not seem like the thing for me.

While being a minister of the gospel, was never what I imagined for myself, God had another plan. He started conditioning my spirit and I began seeing visions of myself preaching. Because I had disbelief, I simply dismissed the visions and imaginations. Though I continued to dismiss and ignore, the visions kept showing up in my mind and spirit. It got to the point, that my spirit became restless, and it was all I could think about. Nevertheless, I still did not believe and dismissed it all. It got so bad, that I had to talk to my pastor about it all. He informed me that I should yield to God and pray that God would reveal to me what He had in store. But my pastor was certain that this was God trying to get my attention and tell me something.

Naturally, I prayed. But my prayer was not that God would reveal, instead I prayed that He would stop the visions and give me peace of mind. Because I was determined to fight with God about what He was doing in my life, He had to take a "once-and-for-all" stance with me. One night at three in the morning, God awakened me from my sleep and spoke so clearly to me that I would almost swear I heard Him as clearly audibly as I did spiritually. He told me that the visions and imaginations were not just my own imaginations or strange thoughts, but they were indeed planted in my spirit by Him. He confirmed loud and clear that it was His plan for me to preach the gospel and He had anointed me to do so.

After this, I stepped out on faith and embraced my calling. From that point, sixteen years ago, I have grown in my ministry and preaching. I am serving in my second pastorate with a thriving ministry and church. Since overcoming disbelief and walking in my calling, I have been blessed tremendously. The greatest blessing is being used by God to bless others through His word.

The Challenge

1.  Examine yourself to see if there is something that you just can not get out of your spirit.

2.  Talk to your spiritual leader to get help understanding.

3.  Pray and ask God to show you His plan or calling for your life.

4.  Ask God to help you exercise your faith and help your unbelief.

5.  Believe what Philippians 4:13 says in that you can do all things through Christ…

# CHAPTER THREE

...................................................................................................

# CONTENTMENT

Contentment is an interesting fight to have with God. If you are at a place where you are content with what you have. You are not hurting for anything. There is really nothing that you want or need. With this being the case, and somehow you are still fighting with God. It seems like an unfair fight. It is almost as if God is picking the fight and bothering you when you really want to just walk away and be left alone. This is exactly right. It is natural for everyone to get to a place in their life where they plateau. Where everything is smooth and quiet. This is the point where most people want to coast and take it easy.

On the flip side of things, you may be one of those individuals who sells yourself short and never accomplish anything. And unfortunately, are completely content with that. Those who feel this way, apparently misinterpret what the Apostle Paul stated in Philippians 4:11-12. As he states he has learned to be content with having little or having much. But Paul was not stating this conclusively as he is content with staying at having little or much. But he is saying that when he has little, he is content because he still has God and God will increase him. As well, when he has much, he is content, because he still has God who gave it to him and can give him more. So, the contentment is not so much with the things, but with the God who gave them.

This is how God operates. As long as you are alive, there is still more for you to do and to receive. Since you have surrendered to God, you no longer get to say when enough is enough. Even if you are at place in your life where you are totally and completely comfortable. God is always in control and only He gets to decide when enough is enough. God is a perpetual God. He never stops moving. Some people have a misconception of the scripture in the book of Genesis when it says that on the seventh day God rested. Many would take this to mean that God actually sat down and did absolutely nothing for a whole day. Not so. If this were true, then Psalm 121:4 would not make sense. It says that God never slumbers or sleeps. So clearly, God did not do nothing on the seventh day. What he actually did was stop creating things, for everything he desired had been created. So instead of doing nothing for a whole day, He continued to govern and sustain what He had created. In essence, He stood back and worshiped himself.

This is what God is doing with you, even though you are trying to rest on contentment. When God created you, yes, you were good. However, God is ever trying to make you better.

Better as a person

Better in ministry

Better in relationships

Better in your career

You do not stop at the place where you feel you are good enough. But God had a plan for you before you were formed and He can not stop until He fulfills the plan He has.

Again, you have to be aware that God is ultimately in control of your life and he created you from the beginning with this in mind.

> *Jeremiah 29:11 (NKJV) "For I know the plans I have for you, says the Lord. They are plans for good and not for disaster, to give you a future and a hope."*

God fully holds the plans for your life in His hands. It is wonderful to set goals for your life. To make plans for your life. To have dreams and aspirations for your life. You should do all these things and you should strive with everything in you to accomplish them. However, you cannot leave God out of your plans. In fact, you must seek God out to see what His plans are for you and then wrap your plans around or intertwine them with his. If you do not do this, you will go through life accomplishing everything you set your heart to and still feel empty at the end of the day. The emptiness comes from the God factor.

So many people find themselves in this predicament in life and it usually leads them to a terrible and sometimes irrevocable state. They don't understand how they can be so successful, yet still feel so under-accomplished. Then to try and cope, they seek other devices to try and fill the void, such as drugs, alcohol, promiscuity and wild adventures. If not these things, then they go into a deep depression and anxiety. None of which are good for them and again, are sometimes irrevocable. Unfortunately, while they try all these alternative methods of seeking solution, they never try the one who has all the answers. That is God our Father through the compassionate, loving savior, Jesus Christ. He is the one who holds all the answers in his hand and is eager to lead you to the place of peace and prosperity for your life.

Those who come out of the stage of confusion and feeling of emptiness and incompletion, find that God gives them the wisdom to understand exactly where they are in their lives and shows them the way out. He does this for them and will also do the same for you. In seeking God, he will help you understand true contentment. In understanding true contentment, you understand according to 1 Timothy 6:6, that godliness with contentment is great gain. This means that the only way to have true contentment is to have your accomplished plans overlapping God's plans for you. This is where great gain is produced. The great gain is joy in your overall well-being. It is where now you are not just feeling accomplished physically and financially, with wealth, possessions and accolades. But you are also feeling accomplished spiritually because you know you have fulfilled God's will for your life. As well, you are accomplished mentally and emotionally because you know you've done everything the right way. There is no guilt or shame. But more than anything, you have a relationship with God that transcends time. It is inseverable and eternal.

As you embrace this relationship with God, the joy and contentment that you feel through Him, gives you direction in life. You understand that your life is not only about you. Grasping this fact, shifts your focus and you no longer look for opportunities in life to please yourself, but you begin looking for ways you can help and benefit others. This is the contentment that God is trying to get you to. The contentment that replicates Jesus' sacrifice on the cross for you and me. The contentment he felt in that he considered it "a joy" to go to the cross for all of mankind. The contentment he felt in that he stated, "no man takes my life, but I lay it down." True contentment is not that you have lived a great life and left everyone else behind. But it is that you have served others through your gifts and talents and made a difference and positive impact on others.

In the wisdom you gain from your relationship with God, you realize the more you achieve and accomplish, the more you need to achieve and accomplish.

> *Luke 12:48 (NKJV) "For everyone to whom much is given, from him much will be required..."*

This verse of scriptures declares that there is no complacency in contentment. It also indicates that you are to do something with what you gain. Not just put it in a trophy case. Or put it in a vault. You can't just be proud of it and make it the topic of conversation at your parties or family gatherings. But as God gives to you and makes provision for your gain, you are to share it with others. No, not just simply give away your valuables and hard-earned money. You may do this from time to time, but I don't mean just feely give up everything you have worked so hard for. But you should share your success stories. You should share the details of your relationship with God and how he can help others get to the level of success that you have obtained. This is what God desires and requires of you. This is the point of your greatest contentment. This is the only true contentment. Anything else will leave you feeling empty.

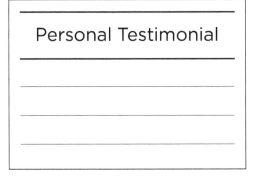

It took me a long time to realize how to understand and manage contentment. I was one of those who thought it was fine to have nothing in life and just be content with having nothing. I looked at my life as having the essential things like food, clothing, and shelter. I thought as long as I had those things and had good health, I was right where I needed to be. I did not need a lot of money, big houses, and fancy cars. I already had a good relationship with God, so I was fine, so I thought. As my relationship grew with God, so did my wisdom and understanding. I learned that I was okay to not seek the money, houses, and cars. But the knowledge of God and his word, were more valuable than any of those things or anything else in life. It was the knowledge of him and his word that God was giving me and what brought me the greatest contentment. Then in sharing his word and his wisdom with others, as he required, in return it brought me gain in finances as well. I literally got to experience God fulfilling his word of Luke 12:48 in my life. The more I was content to give through Him, the more He gave to me.

Needless to say, I was no longer content to live a mediocre life, but I was striving to gain more through God. The reason was not to have a bunch of stuff, to put in a trophy case, or vault, or make the topic of conversation, but it was to share with others. I wanted more so I could give more. This was how I gained contentment. For I knew I was able to be a blessing to others and more-so I knew that God could trust me to do what was right with anything and everything He gave to me.

---

## The Challenge

---

1. Examine yourself to see how content you are at this point in life.

2. Ask yourself what makes you feel content.

3. If God is not a part of your life, have you ever felt emptiness even in your contentment?

4. Consider establishing a relationship with God to fulfill your joy.

5. Begin sharing with others for the sake of God and see if your emptiness is replaced with true contentment and greater rewards.

# CHAPTER FOUR

# REBELLION

This entire book is basically dealing with rebellion. The fact that you are not allowing God to have full and total control of your life as He desires, is rebellion. Rebellion is your trying to do everything your way. It is you trying to fulfill the plan for your life without fully knowing what the plan is. Only God knows the complete plan for your life. However, He is not selfish with it. In fact, He wants to share it with you. As a matter of fact, as it relates to your life, there is nothing more that God wants to do for you, than share His plan for your life, and help you fulfill it. The reason is because to know God's plan for your life requires you to communicate with Him. In communication with Him you draw close to Him. As you draw close to Him, you develop relationship with Him. In relationship with Him, there is closeness and even one-ness. When you look at this scenario in totality, now both you and God are happy because you're both getting what you desire. And as the common phrase goes, "life is good".

What I just described is ideal and ultimate. Unfortunately, for most, this scenario is not the case. There are too many people who are not walking in peace and harmony with God, but are in fact, in rebellion. This rebellion comes in one or both of two forms. First, this rebellion is brought on by a lack of faith and trust in God to know that He has the plan for your life. The other is the just pure disobedience and disregard for God.

To have a lack of faith and trust in God is very common. It does not mean that you are a bad person, or that you are just a terrible "sinner". Sometimes when you do not have complete faith and trust in God is because you have not grown or matured to that level yet. Perhaps you are a new convert who just took the walk of faith with God and are feeling your way through. Or maybe you've just started attending church and are still learning and taking your time trying to understand how things work. You have not accepted Christ yet, but you are working your way toward it. You may be surprised to know that everyone who is a regular attendee of church is not walking in complete faith and trust with God. It takes longer for some people to get to this point than it does for others. As well, life experiences also play a role in getting you to this place with God. There is an old saying that says "some people don't pray until they get in trouble". As bad as this sounds, there is some amount of truth to it. When you have a regard for God, sometimes, you don't seek to strengthen your relationship with Him until you fall on tough times. You may not consider it in this way, but this is a form of rebellion. It is you saying "I'm going to retain control of the situations of my life until they get out of hand. Then I'll call on God to help me if I need it. While you may be struggling through the crises of your life, God is standing by thinking "if only he would allow me to help him". Not only does God feel hurt and left out because of your rebellion, be He also feels pain for you in having to watch you suffer when you don't have to. With God there is no shared responsibility. He has full responsibility for your life. And when you let Him, He directs you step by step through every stage, according to the plan He has already laid out. But you must trust Him and let Him have total control.

> *Luke 9:23 (NKJV) "If anyone desires to come after Me, let him deny himself, and take up his cross daily, and follow Me".*

In this passage, Jesus is making a stern and clear declaration of what is required to have a right relationship with Him. It takes a strong stance against you living in rebellion. He clearly says if you are going to walk with Him, you must deny yourself. This obviously means that you cannot be in control. You must let Jesus have total control. Anything else is rebellion. Along with that, Jesus explains that walking with Him is not easy but it's worth it. He says you must take up your cross daily. The reference to the cross is the fact that Jesus had to endure suffering and anguish to absolve the debt of sin that mankind did, does, and will, indulge in. Jesus is saying that if you are going to follow Him, you must be willing to suffer through the temptations to rebel and do wrong, trying to handle things yourself, in order that you might do what is right, let Him have control and live righteously with Him. This requires strong faith and trust. Yet, it is much easier than living in rebellion and suffering through life trying to figure everything out yourself.

Living in rebellion because you have not grown or matured to that point, is one thing. However, when you live in rebellion because of sheer disobedience and disregard for God is totally another. This situation is much more severe and can be much more costly in the long run. Possibly even to the point of costing you your life. This does not mean that God is going to just kill you. It means that when you totally disregard God, you are fully without His provision and protection. Everything that happens in your life must be dealt with by yourself. You do have God's grace, but there are times when your grace period runs out. In those times, you could find yourself in a situation where you go too far and put yourself in an irrevocable situation that you cannot recover from. At this point, God will turn you over to the reprobate of your own mind.

Disregard for God is a serious indictment. It means you are operating in or at the brink of blasphemy, which says you deny even the reality of God. This sin is one God cannot forgive, according to Matt. 12:31. This is not only lifelong damnation, but eternal damnation. I pray you are not someone like this. This is a very serious matter that requires immediate attention. There is no recovering from this and while you think you can handle it, or are willing to take your chances, I strongly advise against it. In this severe case of rebellion and disregard for God, there is dire consequences. However, in another disregard for God, the consequences are not quite as severe, but damaging, nonetheless. What I'm referring to is idolatry. Idolatry is not like blasphemy where there is a complete denial of the existence of God. Idolatry, on the other hand, is being so into yourself that you make yourself equal with God. In many cases of idolatry, you have made a good life for yourself. You graduated high school and college. Because of your degree, you got a great job or career. You made thousands or even millions of dollars. Your family is doing well. Spouse is equally as successful and savvy. "Life is good"! With all this power and accomplishments, you begin to rely on all your success and accolades. You start to credit your success with you being the great person you are. While you are wrapped up in yourself, you lose sight of God and diminish the thought of needing Him in your life. You think "I've made it this far and done this well without him". "Why do I need to go to church"? "I have several academic degrees, what can anyone at the church teach me"? All of these are sure signs of rebellion in the form of idolatry. You are not like the blasphemer in that you deny God is real. No, you acknowledge God is real, you just do not see a need for Him in your life. In being idolatrous, you indirectly make yourself equal with God as a god of your own life. You may not want to think of it this way, but when you acknowledge the fact that God created you, to completely disregard Him and give Him place in your life, is saying you are your own god.

God frowns on this behavior as this is one of the ten commandments; "you shall have no other gods before me". This includes:

yourself…

your job…

your money…

your car…

your home…

your degrees…

your spouse…

your children, etc…Anything you place more reverence on or put more emphasis on than the true and living God becomes your god.

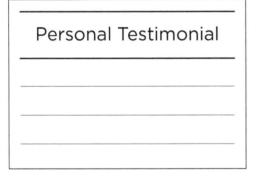

I would say that for my entire childhood, I was rebellious. My mother would probably call it hard-headed. I was a "what-if" child. So, anything my mother told me not to do, I always had in the back of my mind "well, what if I did it anyway"? For the most part, this was regarding harmless things that would not destroy my life or kill me. However, it did get me a few lashes to my backside. Obviously, we can't do that with children today, but it was the cultural norm, forty-plus years ago. And let's face it, I'm writing this book so apparently it didn't kill me. As a matter of fact, it helped me.

Being rebellious with parents is fairly common with all children, but things get to be much more serious when we are rebellious toward God. Unfortunately, I must admit that there was a point in my life where I was rebellious toward God as well. I went through a mild depression in my early teen years, and I was very angry most of the time. I didn't like the fact that I was poor and had a dim outlook on my future. Obviously, at this age, I knew of God but hadn't grown to trust him for the betterment of my life. I felt that all I had was me, so that's who I trusted and depended on. When I was fifteen, I started working part-time while in high school. This was great for me. I now had money that I could buy the clothes and shoes that my mother couldn't afford, due to living on disability and raising three other kids. I could buy myself a car. I really thought I had it going on at this point. Since things were now going well, I continued this lifestyle for the next five years or so. Even working my way through college, I had a job while I continued to work and make money.

To make matters worse, looking good and having a car, and getting a college education, drew the attention of females. I started having my way with females and things were good. I really didn't love or even care much for them, for I was only into myself. Yes, this was rebellion of the worst kind. I was living life how I wanted to and thought it was going well, until people started getting hurt. I was so into myself that it never dawned on me that I was hurting others. Believe it or not, I never meant to hurt anyone as I was not an evil person. I just wanted to make myself happy. Certainly, this is not what God wanted for me or the people I hurt.

When the realization of hurting others set in, guess what else came back. Yes, the depression. It was as if I had gone from the ditch on one side of the road all the way over to the one on the other side. I needed to find my way to the middle of the road. How do I do this? I was too ashamed to go and talk to a therapist because of the stigma on seeing therapists. By the way, I didn't know then, but if you don't see a therapist when you need to, you are being ridiculous… So, what would I do?

I had been given a bible for Christmas the previous year and I decided I would sit down and start reading it. It was a Wednesday night and I had finished my shift at work. I took a bath and sat on the side of my bed and began reading. I was reading the book of Romans and for whatever reason, I started in chapter 8. The first verse said there is no condemnation to them who are in Christ Jesus. This gave me hope and interest to continue reading. Then I read that all things work together for good to those who love God and are called according to His purpose. As I continue to read, tears begin to flow. And by the time I got to chapter 10 I was weeping like a baby. I surrendered my life to Christ and confessed from my mouth my profession of faith that I believe Jesus is the son of God and Risen Savior of the world. I went to the church the following Sunday and made it official and began my journey with God. This was twenty-six years ago, and I must say that since I stopped rebelling against God and trusted Him with my life, it has been a beautiful journey. Life has been filled with the greatest blessings that I could never have accomplished on my own.

## The Challenge

1. Examine yourself and see how you may be in rebellion towards God.

2. Are there areas of your life where you have not totally surrendered to God?

3. How often do you read the bible?

4. Do you have a therapist or church counselor that you can talk to about what's going on in your life?

5. Are you hurting yourself and/or others because you refuse to seek help, especially from God?

# CHAPTER FIVE

# FEAR

Operating in fear is quite possibly the biggest fight with God that you can enter into. Fear is debilitating and paralyzing. It is so broad that it shadows your life in so many different ways. Worst of all, fear is a weapon that the evil one uses to keep you from flourishing and being successful in life. So imagine, being under a powerful influence of satan, while God is still trying to pull you in the direction of freedom and safety. When you give in to fear, your life is essentially put on hold. You can't do anything even for yourself, and certainly can't do anything for God. Surrendering to fear robs you of life.

You may be wondering right now, "how can I overcome fear when there are truly things that I am afraid of?" You have to understand that you are in full control of fear. It does not control you. Sure there are hundreds or even thousands of things in life that you can be afraid of. For instance, bears or wild animals. Some people are afraid of snakes or spiders. Then there are people who are afraid of heights. I could go on and on, but the point is all these things are natural. All of these are things that can truly harm you and you should be very cautious of them in certain settings. But just having phobias or fear of specific things that can harm you is not the essence of fear. The true essence of fear is when you hold yourself back for the fear of what might or might not happen. It is basically the hindrance of your actions based on the unknown.

If you decide to not go into the woods because there are bears there that might attack you, that is not so much fear as it is wisdom. If you choose not to climb to the top of Mt. Everest or go zip-lining above tree tops in a Mexican forest, for fear that you might fall, that is understandable. This is perfectly normal. But what is not normal is the fear of succeeding. The fear of failing. The fear to exercise your spiritual gifts and flow in the anointing of God. It is not normal or healthy for you to not indulge in something because you are afraid of what people might think. Or you fear that you might not be good at it. You should also not withhold yourself from something because you're afraid it will be more than you can handle. As well, you should not be afraid to try something because you have never done it before and it seems strange or awkward to you.

It sounds cliché but you have to get yourself to a point in life where you operate in faith over fear. There are many things that God wants for your life, but you must have the faith to carry those things out without fear. If you are afraid of living by God's plan, you will never achieve your fullest potential in life. Remember, God knows more about you than you know about yourself. When you can overcome fear and trust Him, He will do great and mighty things through and for you. More than that, you will in-turn feel empowered, bold, and fulfilled. You will feel like the conqueror that you are in God.

> *2 Timothy 1:7 (NKJV) "For God has not given us a spirit of fear, but of power and of love and of a sound mind".*

In this passage, we are being convinced that if we have a spirit of fear that it did not come from God. Just as I mentioned earlier, it is natural to be afraid of things that can harm you. But this is not a spirit of fear. It is a natural awareness of things that are more powerful and fierce than you are, which you are very unlikely to overcome. However, a spirit of fear is that paralyzing and debilitating spirit that comes over you to hinder you from fulfilling the will of God for your life. It is an evil spirit that does not want you to have a healthy relationship with God. It does not want you to please God. If does not want you to succeed or achieve your dreams and desires for yourself. This spirit of fear has to be overcome so that you can stop fighting with God for your success.

The scripture even shares with you that God is trying to help you put down the weapon of fear and trust Him to lead you. It says that instead of the spirit of fear, God actually gave you the power to overcome it. Remember that you were created in the image and likeness of God. You were shaped and molded in His spirit and nature. Because you have God's nature, you have the ability or power to overcome any opposing spirit that would seek to overtake you. When you choose to use God's power and overcome fear, you stop fighting with God and you actually turn the fight to the one who you should be fighting and that is satan.

Not only does the scripture state that you have power, but also love. This love covers a multitude of sins you could or would commit against God. Because you love God, you can trust Him and know that He is for you and not against you. The love for God causes you to want to please Him. The love of God also makes you love yourself. When you love yourself, it drives you to want the best for yourself. If you want the best for yourself, you can overcome fear to achieve it, especially when you know and love God who you realize can help you do it. Love is a powerful thing. This is why it is mentioned over five hundred times in the bible. It is necessary to have a great life.

Finally the scripture teaches we are given sound mind or stable thinking. Peace of mind also comes along with this. Having a clear and uncluttered mind keeps you focused. You can focus on the task at hand. You can focus on achieving the goals for your life and the will of God, instead of dreading the fear of how you think things will or will not turn out. When you have a sound mind, it also gives you a peace to know that when you are carrying out God's will you don't have to worry because he is making all things work together for your good because you love Him. Experience also comes along with this peace. The experience you gain through every circumstance that God sees you through gives peace of mind and courage to go forth with the next challenge or phase of life. Because you know what God did for you before you have no doubts that He will also come through for you in the next challenge.

Whenever I think about fear, I can't help but think about David in the bible, and when he went out to fight Goliath. Everyone else in the town was afraid of Goliath because he was a giant. He stood tall over everyone else. He was strong and had a history of all the victims he had fought and destroyed previously. No one wanted to face off with Goliath. Until one day, this little shepherd boy, David, heard the news of this tyrant who was wreaking havoc on the town. So he decided to go out and fight the giant. Understand that David didn't just voluntarily go out to fight, but he knew it was God's will that he do so. As the story goes, David went forth without armor or shield and with only a sling-shot. With one sling of a stone he hit Goliath right in the head and killed him.

There are a number of things that manifest in our lives as giants, which we could be fearful of. But the question is, will you succumb to fear or will you have the faith to trust God and fight your giants? Will you fight God by resisting his will for fear, or will you fight and conquer your giants knowing that God is with you and will cause you to triumph?

## Personal Testimonial

The thought of fear almost makes me afraid. There are so many things I used to be afraid of. I was afraid of the dark. I was afraid of flying in a plane. I was even afraid of drowning in water. All of these are very common but the worst fear I had was of failure. I quickly came to realize that this fear of failure was robbing me of living my best life. Failure for me went deeper than not scoring a good grade on a test, or not making the basketball team. But failure for me, meant not succeeding in life with all the things that I wanted to accomplish. Failing for me, meant I wasn't good enough to be great. So, this fear was paralyzing. It caused me not to try to do any of the things that I really wanted to do in life because in my mind, I wasn't good enough and it wasn't going to work out well.

Even when I decided to write a book, fear set in on me and I started thinking that it was not possible for me to write a book. No one in my family had ever written one, I didn't have that type of background or up-bringing. Why would I try to do this? Then I remembered the scripture in 2 Timothy 1:7. I decided that I would overcome my fear by trusting God. If God didn't give me this spirit of fear, then why am I allowing it to control my life. I then remembered what the Apostle Paul said in Philippians 4:13, that I can do all things through Christ Jesus who gives me strength and ability. Needless to say, having this powerful reinforcement of scripture, I went on to write my first book, "Marriage That Lasts" and it was a success and blessing to all who read it. But that wasn't the stopping point, I also wrote a second book for children, "2020, What A Year" and now you are currently reading my third writing.

So, I encourage you to never doubt yourself and get overcome with fear. If God is for you, He is more that the whole world against you. There are a multitude of gifts and talents inside of you that are being blocked by your fear. Do as I did and meet your fear head on with the determination to be successful and a strong trust in God. Hopefully one day I will be seeing your work published and displayed for the world to see.

---

## The Challenge

---

1. Examine yourself and determine what you fear the most?

2. Ask yourself "do you want to live your whole life in fear?

3. How much do you trust God?

4. Can you overcome your fear to accomplish what you want in life?

5. Begin taking small steps to overcome smaller things first then move on to tackling the bigger issues of fear.

6. God wants to help you overcome fear. Stop fighting with Him by letting fear control your life.

# CHAPTER SIX

# RESENTMENT AND REMORSE

L et's face it, everyone has done something they are not particularly proud of or are ashamed of. This is common with every human being. No one is perfect, and in most cases, you have to make mistakes before you learn how to get things right. As it has been said "Experience is the best teacher". However, to recover from your mistakes and mishaps, you must submit yourself to being a student of them and learning from them. If you don't, there is a great chance that you will continue doing the same thing over and over again. This cycle of stress and dissatisfaction wears you down and robs you of life. You begin to lose hope of ever being happy. You stop caring about yourself and abandon any effort of doing the right thing. Life begins to crumble at your feet and you give up.

This is not the way anyone should have to live. It is certainly not the way that God wants you to live. If this is your life, then you are definitely in competition or a fight with God. God desires for you to live life more abundantly and if this is your plight, it's time to turn things around. Part of living with resentment and remorse is due to living in the past. You cannot live in the past and the future at the same time. To move forward with life, you must embrace the present and strive for the future. The present is just that. It is a gift from God for getting through your past. The past is exactly what it is. It has already passed and gone. You cannot change it and you can't undo it. The only thing you can do with your past is to learn from it. Again, if you survived it, then you have received the gift of the "present". If you allow the things you did in your past to hold you hostage, you will never have the blessings of your future.

Your resentment might not be exactly from things you have done. Oftentimes, we hold resentment towards others for the things they have done to us. As sure as you have done things to hurt others, you have also been the victim of being hurt by others. Truthfully, it is a lot easier to get over what you did to someone than it is to overcome what has been done to you. Just saying it seems odd, because it gives the impression that what you did to another was not as bad as what was done to you. It seems as if you deserve to be forgiven and whoever hurt you does not. When it is put in this perspective, what is the right answer or proper approach? Well, one thing is for sure, if you are having this battle in your mind or emotions, then you are fighting with God. God does not want you perplexed over what you have done or what has been done to you. He certainly does not want you to hold resentment or ill-will toward another person. This goes directly against kingdom principles.

God wants us to love one another and help each other so His kingdom can be strengthened. For this to happen, there must be forgiveness. This is a tough word and an even tougher action. God is the best example of having to forgive. He must forgive all day every day. He must forgive those who deny Him, who disobey Him, who persecuted and wrongfully prosecuted His Son Jesus. So yes, God knows about forgiveness. If you are going to overcome the resentment and remorse of your life, you too, must forgive. I don't know what was done to you or by whom, but I do know that if you want to stop being a victim to it, you must forgive the one who hurt you. Unforgiveness is an overwhelming cage. If you won't forgive those who hurt you, you remain trapped in the cage of the emotions, memories, and terror of the situation. If you would only forgive, then the curse is broken. You are set free to enjoy your life. I must agree it is not easy to do, but you can do it with God's help.

The first step is seeking forgiveness from God for the things you have done to others and against God.

> *1 John 1:9 (NKJV) "If we confess our sins, He is faithful and just to forgive us our sins and to cleanse us for all unrighteousness".*

To enable yourself to forgive others, you must admit the fact that you are no more perfect than they are. To admit that you have committed sins and done wrong just like anyone else. This is not for the other person, but for God. He needs to confirm that you acknowledge your faults and flaws that were unpleasing to Him. He then proceeds with forgiving you so that you can proceed with forgiving others. How hypocritical would it be of God to help you forgive others and never get you to deal with the wrong that you have done. God wants to heal you, but he also wants to heal others from you. It all works together. He can't heal them until they forgive you and He can't heal you until you forgive them. God wants everyone to be healed.

> *Ephesians 4:32 (NKJV) "be kind to one another, tenderhearted, forgiving one another, even as God in Christ forgave you".*

God wants everyone to be forgiven and to heal from the hurts and wrongs committed against them during their lives. As you can see, we are all in this together. We are all God's children, and He wants the best for everyone. He does not make differences in the sins, or the actions committed. He doesn't state how one action is worst than another. In his eyes, if your action offended another, it doesn't matter if you murdered someone or just cut them off in traffic. It's all the same to Him. You see, with God it is not about the action, but about how it made the other person feel or respond. He wants unity and harmony amongst His children. Any action that defies this God counts as an offense and requires it to be rectified. He takes this so seriously that if you don't do it, He halts the progress of your life.

> *Matthew 6:14-15 (NKJV) "For if you forgive men their trespasses, your heavenly Father will forgive you. But if you do not forgive men their trespasses, neither will your Father forgive your trespasses".*

If you have unconfessed wrong or sin in your life that you have not been forgiven for, then the blessings of your life are halted. God wants to bless you with abundant life, but you are blocking your blessings if you cannot forgive others. This is a requirement of God. Some might say it this way, "God can't bless mess". Wherever there is mess in your life, whether you created it, or it was shoveled upon you, if it is not cleared up through forgiveness, God can't bless you like He wants to. So maybe this is the answer to why you have felt that you can't get your breakthrough. It could be as simple as dealing with a situation in your life where you need to forgive someone or ask for forgiveness for something you have done.

Perhaps your issue with forgiveness is not something that deals with resentment or what someone did to you. Perhaps it deals more with remorse and what you did to another. You're not fighting with God for Him to help you forgive another, instead you are fighting with God for Him to help you forgive yourself. Sure, God wants to forgive you and wants you to forgive yourself, but you don't feel that you should be forgiven. You don't think you deserve to be forgiven. You think what you did is so bad that it is impossible for even God to forgive you and therefore you can't forgive yourself. This is the worst possible imprisonment. Self-imprisonment inflicted by the thoughts of your mind and the emotion of your heart is the most difficult to be released from. I say to you again, there is nothing that Jesus can't forgive.

*Luke 23:34 (NKJV) "Then Jesus said, Father, forgive them for they do not know what they do".*

Jesus spoke these words while he was nailed on the cross of crucifixion for his death. Mind you, He had done no wrong to deserve this most cruel and awful punishment delivered to man. Prior to this stage of his death sentence, He was mocked, humiliated, beaten, spit on, and forced to carry up the hill, the very cross to which He was nailed. Nevertheless, He looked upon the crowed of those who did this to Him and declared these words of forgiveness. Surely, if Jesus could forgive those who performed such a terrible, heinous, and unjustified act to Him, you can forgive offences committed toward you and by you. Believe me, I know it is not easy, but it is very possible. The whole reason for Jesus going through The Cross was for sins to be forgiven. This means for you to forgive yourself as well. If you have confessed your sin or issue to Jesus with a sincere and repentant heart, and have changed and no longer committing the fault, then Jesus has forgiven you. So, if He has forgiven you, release yourself from your prison of remorse and resentment by forgiving yourself and move on enjoying your life. By living with the resentment and remorse, you are fighting against God and fighting against yourself. So technically, you are fighting a losing battle all the way around. You have absolutely no chance of a good life. But if you let it go, you get release from God then He helps you release yourself.

∞

## Personal Testimonial

In my life I have had some major hurts. In the time when I was a child I was picked on and teased. In today's terms you would probably say I was bullied. I was picked on because of how I looked. Apparently, I looked funny or weird as a child. I was picked on because of being poor and not having the nice clothes, shoes, and possessions that other kids had. I was even picked on because of how I talked. I always had a slightly higher pitch to my voice before puberty set in. And I also had a small lisp that didn't allow me to pronounce words correctly. You might say that this was typical children behavior, but it didn't feel that way to me. You see, you never know how what you say or do affects others. While you may think it is completely harmless, you could be doing a great deal of harm to the person.

I also dealt with resentment and remorse because of things I did to others. During those late teen years and early twenties, I caused a lot of hurt to many people. I felt that I didn't deserve to be forgiven for much of it and that landed me in a dark place. Believe it or not, it was much easier for me to forgive than to allow myself to be forgiven. The funny thing is, I have always held myself to a higher standard and hurting people was not permissible at all. I somewhat expected to be hurt and disappointed by others, but I never wanted to hurt anyone else. So, when I accepted the realization that I had hurt others, it was the worst thing possible for me. I could hardly believe it was me who had done those things. Obviously, it was very difficult for me to forgive myself and I struggled with it for a long while.

Fortunately for me, I had people in my life who also knew that I was not the bad person who had done the bad things. They counseled me and told me about Jesus. How everything that happens in life has a purpose to it. They told me how Jesus knows everything that is going on with me and He will forgive me. I took their advice and began striving to learn and know more about Jesus. As I gained knowledge and faith, I ultimately surrendered my life to Him. I obviously asked him to forgive me of all my sins and he did. Miraculously, I was also able to forgive myself of the sins and wrong that I had committed as well as forgive everyone else who wronged me.

I am overjoyed that I found this newness of life through Jesus Christ, or else I wouldn't be the person I am today. Nor would I have the wonderful life that I live. Breaking the chains of bondage from resentment and remorse helped me end this fight with God. I was holding myself back while He was trying to move me forward.

The Challenge

1. Examine your heart for resentment and remorse.

2. Are there people that you have not forgiven for whatever reason?

3. Do you have things that you have not yet asked God to forgive you of?

4. Are you having trouble forgiving yourself for things that you have done or said?

5. Think how many blessings for your life you might be hindering because of unforgiveness?

6. Do you want to be free to live life abundantly, or do you want to spend the rest of your life in the cage of resentment and remorse?

# CHAPTER SEVEN

## SLOTHFULNESS

You may wonder how slothfulness is a fight against God. Matter of fact, you might even be wondering, "What exactly is slothfulness"? Slothful is a fight against God because it means that one is lazy, has no drive or motivation. It means that you lack aggression. It means that you are slow to move or act on an opportunity, so you often miss out and don't get what was meant for you in that particular situation or season of your life. God moves in seasons, and there are times when the season comes around that God is ready to manifest a blessing of favor in your life. However, because you are slow to move or react, you miss it. Sometimes if you're fortunate, the season will roll back around, but sometimes it was only meant for that time and it is completely gone. This is a fight between you and God. He is diligently trying to manifest greatness in your life, and you continue to ride the slow boat of mediocrity.

Remember when you were a child or maybe even have small children now. Children have to constantly be urged to move and get going. Even with getting out of bed, as a child your parents had to tell you multiple times get up, wash your face, brush your teeth, and get ready for school. The first time never worked, you had to be told again and again before you got up to get moving. This was only the beginning. Once you finally got off to school, some of your teachers had to do the same thing with you at school. Having to constantly urge you to participate in class. Often-times having to send notes home to your parents because you were not performing well. Unfortunately, this behavior continued after you returned home from school. Now you're having to be forced to do your homework. Your parents had to remind you that you were on a time schedule. Homework had to be done before play time. After play time you had to eat dinner then a bath. After the bath, you had to get to bed to so that the routine could start all over again the next morning. Granted, this might have been the exception and not the norm for some children, but for most, this was the daily routine.

The primary issue with this scenario is this behavior carries from childhood into adulthood. You are likely that one who even as an adult you have this slothful spirit and for whatever reason, still can't get moving and get your life on track. Imagine how your parents felt when you were a child, and they were constantly dealing with you about this lackluster nature. Well, I can tell you that Jesus feels now, exactly how your parents felt then. Our Savior is fighting with you every day to move you out of this slow motion and get you moving aggressively toward the life He has planned for you. In order for you to receive everything God has in store for you through Jesus Christ, there must be a parallel pattern of following along with Jesus. There must be a matching aggression to keep up with Him. He has already laid the plan, and is ready to guide you in it, but you must get moving. To know our Heavenly Father, you will understand that He is mindful of timing. For Him, the Trinity (Father, Son, Holy Spirit) is eternal, so time is nothing to Him. He transcends time. However, for you, you are bound by time. You will only live so long. Worst of all, you don't know how long. Therefore, it is so critical that you grab hold of God with a strong grip and desire and live the great life He wants for you.

> *Matthew 11:12 (NKJV) "And from the days of John the Baptist until now the kingdom of heaven suffers violence, and the violent take it by force."*

This profound and often misunderstood scripture speaks to how God wants us to overcome our slothful spirit. Jesus is teaching that the power of the Kingdom of heaven is under attack. Obviously, there were human and spiritual forces working against Jesus who is the embodiment of the Kingdom of heaven. But He was also saying that there was a hindrance against the Kingdom trying to prevent others from being a part of it. So, there was a great need for those who were already of the Kingdom, or faithful believers in Christ Jesus, to work diligently to continue to advance the Kingdom of heaven. In advancing the Kingdom of heaven, they would therefore also make life better for themselves.

Then the violence and violent that this scripture proclaims, is not necessarily speaking of physical war. It is more so speaking of spiritual warfare. Jesus is saying to you that you must operate by faith to stand and uphold the doctrine of the Kingdom and the strength of the spiritual power of God. By doing so, you can overcome every obstacle and hindrance in life that would come against you individually or the Kingdom as a whole. In order for you to live the abundant life that is guaranteed through Jesus, you must be aggressive in showing forth your spiritual nature to press through to victory over every circumstance. You don't have to physically kill or fight anyone, you must only avoid being conformed to the world's system and strive to live by faith through Jesus Christ. You must achieve when they say you can't. You continue to speak when they try to shut you up. You must get back up and keep going when they say it's over for you. It is imperative that you be the example of "greater is He that is in me, than he that is in the world". These are reasons why you cannot be slothful. If you are slothful, you will perish. You will struggle through life and ultimately be consumed by the enemy.

> *Proverbs 6:6-12 (NKJV) "Go to the ant, you sluggard!*
> *Consider her ways and be wise, which having no*
> *captain, Overseer or ruler, provides her supplies in*
> *the summer and gathers her food in the harvest. How*
> *long will you slumber, O sluggard? When will you rise*

*from your sleep? A little sleep, a little slumber, a little folding of the hands to sleep, so shall your poverty come on you like a prowler, and your need like an armed man".*

This scripture sums it all up. Solomon, the wisest man in the world wrote this Proverb warning against slothfulness. He makes the comparison to the ant, one of the smallest insects. Though the ant is small, it is very industrious. She has no one to lead her or have rule over her. Yet she is wise to take advantage of the seasons whereby she works diligently in the summer and gathers in the harvest or winter when there no more growth or production. She is also very strong, which allows her to lift and carry things up to twenty times their own weight. According to the average human body weight, if we could lift twenty times our weight, that would be about 4000 pounds. That is around the weight of a small car. But because the ant knows how critical here survival is, she musters up the courage and the stamina to do what's needed to provide for herself and her family, even her community.

This is the same requirement God has for you. Verse nine in this passage asks the question. How long will you slumber? If you slumber too long, you get too comfortable in it until you are virtually comatose to life and all that is going on around you. It is at this point that the prowler of poverty and the armed robber of life overtake you. Why let this happen when God has promised you life more abundantly through Jesus Christ. Jesus has done his part in sacrificing Himself that you may have this abundantly life. Now, it is time for you to stop fighting against Him and embrace it. On that note, even when Jesus was going through life and ultimately to His Cross experience, he wasted no time. He was diligent about it. He was meticulous in that He would not let anything happen before it was time. But when it was time, He acted expediently to complete the task. You cannot be slothful in living a life to which you do not know the ending point. You must take full advantage of every day and optimize every opportunity afforded to you.

In addition, you must also be fully aware of who you serve. There are those who find themselves in a state of slothfulness because they feel undervalued or underappreciated. To evolve in life and never receive commendation from others can dampen your spirit and cause you to quit or give up. But you cannot find yourself in a subservient position to another human being. Everything you do, must be to the glory of God.

> *Colossians 3:23-24 (NKJV) "And whatever you do, do it heartily, as to the Lord and not to men, knowing that from the Lord you will receive the reward of the inheritance, for you serve the Lord Christ".*

The Apostle Paul wrote this in a letter to encourage the Christ-fearing bondservants who were serving their human masters but not receiving just reward from them. He encouraged them to continue to keep their faith in Christ and in everything they do, do it so that Jesus Christ would be pleased. In the end, it will be Christ who makes a way that they would receive their just inheritance and reward. From the treatment the bondservants received from their masters, they could have easily fallen into a slump. Feeling that if you can't appreciate me, I won't work as hard. If you don't value what I do, then I will slack off and not do as much. But Paul encouraged them to do just the opposite. He told them to obey your masters, not with eyeservice, as men-pleasers, but in sincerity of heart, fearing God. Work hard so that God is pleased.

Oh, how I encourage you to have this faith today. To work hard in all you do, not worrying about whether your boss, supervisor, CEO, pastor, friends, spouse, children, parents, or anyone else appreciates it. But that you would work, serve, and do, knowing that it is Christ whom you aim to please. To have the faith, knowing that He sees your tears. He feels your disappointment. He knows all about it. But most importantly, He is counting it as favor unto you. For when you remain faithful to Him, even though others are benefiting from it, yet don't appreciate it, He will elevate you to receive your proper reward. He will either bring them into conformance to your dedication and sacrifice or move you into a better position to be appreciated. Don't be slothful but remain faithful and God is working it out for you. Remember, the fight is not against people, but it is against God. Surrender to God and watch Him turn your life around showing you how to continue glorifying Him through serving ungrateful people, and never lose your joy.

```
_____
      Personal Testimonial
_____
_____
_____
_____
```

I must say that slothfulness has plagued me much of my life. It wasn't so much that I was just lazy and had no desires or intentions, but it was that I was a procrastinator. It took me the longest to ever get started doing something. Even in grade school, with assignments, book reports, special projects, I waited until the last minute to get started. Though I still got it done, I would be frustrated doing it because I would have to stay up late. It would come down to having to do two weeks of work in a manner of hours. I actually scored a good grade on the assignment, but the amount of effort in a short period of time made me tired and angry.

Even to this day, I am much better at controlling the slothfulness or procrastination, but it still lingers. Since I have been living for Christ, I tried to tell myself that it was partly due to my relationship with Him. I thought it was that I needed to be sure it was Christ telling me to do something before I acted upon it. Of course, I was lying to myself. Sure, everyone needs to confirm by faith and in prayer that whatever you have an urge or desire to do, it is Christ who is leading you in it. But don't fool yourself, there is a vast difference in being sure you're led by Christ and just taking forever to get started with something. When you have a solid faith in Jesus Christ, it doesn't take a long time to receive and answer from Him.

I think over the course of my life, there are several blessings that I have missed out on because of slothfulness. Especially in the early years of my life prior to knowing Christ. I didn't have him to charge it to then, so I know it was just me. But I too, fell into the problem of need a strong support group to help me see it through. And not having people in my life who could provide this support made me succumb to the rut of waiting too late to try something, or not doing it at all. Thank God I ended this fight with God and surrendered my life to Him. Since then, I have grown in faith and learned to trust God more. Again, I still deal with the issue daily, but I am more in tune with God and knowing it is Him that I serve. I am fully aware that whatever He requires of me, or I desire to do, if I do it to honor Him, then He has my back.

I have moved beyond what people think or do and have set my mind on being a Kingdom servant. I know that there are those who benefit from what I do, but my full intention and aim is that God is glorified. It did not take me long at all to realize that you can spend your entire life trying to please people and the more you think you please, there are twice as many who are displeased. This is also true with trying to get people to work with you. Many times in my life, I have passed up on opportunities because I was waiting on people to join with me and to their part. Well, it didn't take long for me to see that I couldn't count on people to always be there for me. Either I was going to move forth alone with the task at hand or abandon the effort all together. No doubt, there are many great things I have forfeited in life because of just being lazy or waiting on someone else. But thankfully, God has always provided for me and kept me covered in grace and mercy. Beyond that, He allowed me to learn from my mistakes and gain the wisdom to share with you through my experiences. So don't be overcome by slothfulness and laziness. There is too much that God has in you and in store for you. Stop fighting with Him like I did and since you can't beat Him join Him. I am a living witness that He will bless you with abundant life if you will be aggressive and follow Him by faith.

## The Challenge

1. Examine your life and be honest with yourself regarding laziness or slothfulness.

2. Are you overcome with a spirit of slothfulness?

3. Are you slothful because you lack initiative or creativity?

4. Have you stopped being forceful because no cares or supports you?

5. Can you commit yourself to serving God to please Him only regardless of others?

6. Where would you be in life today, if it weren't for slothfulness or procrastination?

# CHAPTER EIGHT

........................................................................................

# FALSE GODS

·

I t is all too easy to get distracted by something that prevents you from focusing on something that is more important. This happens to most people when it is time to do household chores. Especially if you start in the living room. You need to be going to the storage closet to get the vacuum, but instead you find yourself drawn to the remote control sitting on the coffee table. You know the floor is not going to vacuum itself, but there is this strong desire in you to turn on the TV and watch your favorite show or the game instead. The battle rages within you...watch TV or clean the house? What will you do? Which urge and desire will get the best of you?

This scenario is popularly familiar to everyone. Though it is somewhat innocent and harmless if you forsake cleaning your house to watch TV, it is still a situation of you being distracted by the lesser importance and choosing it over the greater. This won't strike you as critical or condemning, unless you find yourself on one of those TV shows about hoarders who never clean their homes and piles of stuff accumulate around them. However, it is of great significance to you if your very life depended on it.

Imagine, if your spiritual life was focused on the less important things and you always forsake the important. You would be considered a victim of idolizing false gods. Choosing to place more importance on any one thing than you do on the living God through Jesus Christ means you are worshiping false gods. The false gods distract you and keep your attention so that you are unable to focus on harvesting a relationship with God. You would be surprised at how many people are guilty of this but have absolutely no idea that it is even happening in their lives. They know that they don't have a relationship with God, or their relationship with Him is weak, but they don't understand the reason why. Or they think the reason is something altogether different. It is basic human nature that everyone is drawn to something. Most everyone tends to worship or believe in something. It is typically the thing that you love the most. For different people, it is different things, especially if it is not God. But whatever you love, worship, or believe in, you make it your god. This creates a fight between you and the Living God, for He is a jealous God.

> **Exodus 20:5 (NKJV) "You shall not bow down to them nor serve them. For I, the Lord your god, am a jealous God, visiting the iniquity of the fathers upon the children to the third and fourth generations of those who hate Me".**

God issued this command to the children of Israel after He had delivered them from bondage in Egypt. For He declared unto them that they were His children and He loved them so much that He wanted them to only love Him in return. He searched down through many generations seeking out those who succumb to this iniquity of worshiping false gods. You can see He how seriously God takes worship of false gods. He declared He searched the generation of those who hate Him. For God there is no middle ground. There is no gray area. There is no straddling the fence. To God, you either love Him or hate Him. If you're not for Him, you are against Him. It is a shame and frightening that even in this generation of the twenty-first century, there are people who still don't take God seriously.

They choose to go through life with their focus on what pleases them or makes them happy, instead of choosing life with God through Jesus Christ.

Most people don't realize what they've made the focus of their life is a false god. There are several idols that people worship and don't even think twice about it. I could go on for the next several chapters naming all the false gods of people's lives, but I'll only focus on the top three. You may already know what a couple of these are because they might even show a place in your own life.

First, the obvious one is money. True, money is very natural and necessary for life. Everyone needs a certain amount of it, and for whatever reason, no one seems to ever get enough of it. It is a tragedy to spend your entire life chasing money. Especially when you never give God a chance to be Lord of your life. There is a scripture that addresses this concern and unfortunately it is also very widely misinterpreted.

> *1 Timothy 6:10 (NKJV) "For the love of money is a root of all kinds of evil, for which some have strayed from the faith in their greediness and pierced themselves through with many sorrows".*

Although is scripture is very widely mis-quoted and misinterpreted, when properly understood, it is very powerful. Many quote it as saying that money is the root of all evil. However, as you see, it clearly states that the love of money is the root of all evil. Money is just money. It is neither evil nor good. It is what you do to get it or what you do with it when you've got it, that reflects evil or good in you. When you have set your love toward money, you have truly made the money your god. Once money is your god, you have strayed from your faith in the true and living God. This love for money will lead you to performing all kinds of evil acts to get it. Some people sell their bodies to prostitution and stripping. Some sell other people. Money is the reason why human trafficking is so prevalent now. You can even find yourself trying to work two or three jobs to get more money. Doing this destroys your family because you never have time for your children or your spouse. You find yourself facing the second part of this scripture and that is pierced through with many sorrows. You have no peace. You can't sleep at night. Your health starts to fail because you are chasing money and have no time to take care of yourself. Or you're successful in getting money, and you live the wild life enjoying it. You destroy yourself by being surrounded by fast cars, women, drugs and alcohol, or gambling. Just like the prodigal son who is mentioned in Luke chapter 15 of the bible. He lived life on the wild side until he spun out of control and ended up living like the animals. Being broke and having nothing to eat but the scraps from the pig's trough, he realized he had hit rock bottom. Fortunately, for him he decided to call upon his father and go home. But for some, when they hit rock bottom it can lead to more tragic and even fatal consequences like drugs and alcohol to cope. Some even give over to suicide because they can't handle the stress of being broke.

Tearing yourself down trying to get money or living the wild life to splurge on all your money can buy is one thing, but the simple fact that you choose money over God is an act of evil in itself. Any time you choose anything over God, you are operating in evil. You have gained much but profited nothing.

> *Mark 8:36-37 (NKJV) "For what shall it profit a man,*
> *if he shall gain the whole world and lose his own soul?*
> *Or what shall a man give in exchange for his soul"?*

To spend your life gaining money or anything else except a true and wholesome relationship with God, profits you nothing. God is the source of your life. He needs to be the center of your life. Just as gravity keeps you grounded and keeps you from floating around all over the place, God does this for you in a spiritual sense. He keeps your life in balance and keeps you focused on what is important in life and how to prioritize everything about you. Your relationship with God is your true wealth. With God, He can help you get wealth and help you manage and enjoy it. But you cannot serve God and money.

*Matthew 6:24 (NKJV) "No one can serve two masters, for either he will hate the one and love the other or else he will be loyal to the one and despise the other. You cannot serve God and mammon".*

This scripture says it all. You cannot have two masters. You cannot let money be your master and try to serve God effectively. On the flip side, if you choose to serve God as your Heavenly Father, then He can provide you with the wisdom you need to get money and properly manage it. This leads you to a healthy and successful life. A life without stress, worry or sickness. A life surrounded by your family and friends who you now have time to spend with. A life enjoying the finer things without compromising your integrity or your love for God. This is the life God desires for you and you can have it if you stop fighting him by choosing money.

While money is the most obvious idol, there is also a second very prominent false god that you choose over the living God. This false god is family and relationships. It is very easy to get caught up in worshiping your family or spouse, even to the point that you don't realize that you're more into them than you are into God. The reason is because you love them and would do anything in the world for them. You want the best for them, and you dedicate yourself to doing whatever you have to do to meet their needs. You get so used to doing this day after day and before you know it, you have wrapped your life around them. You start feeling like you are not doing something right if you are not doing something for your spouse or your children. Many times, you get frustrated because you start to feel they should be able to take care of themselves. They even show signs that make you think they take you for granted. This is a tell-tell sign that you have made them your god and forsaken Jesus Christ.

Worshiping your family is not just doing something for your family, but it is also just wanting to be with them or around them. This is especially a problem if your family is not into church or have a relationship with God. When you choose to be at family gatherings or get-togethers and never make time to cultivate a relationship with God, you've made them your god. If you spend time with any person or group of people, and they never hold you accountable to have a healthy spiritual life, then they are your false god. Accountability is the key. You want to be around people who are going to help you get connected or strengthen your connection with God. If you do not have people in your life who, first have a relationship with God themselves, then encourage you to do the same, then they are your god.

You don't think of them as being your god because they are family. Obviously, it is natural to love your family and want to spend time with them. This is not a problem. The problem comes in when God is no where in the picture. God must be the most important person in your life above and beyond anyone or anything else.

> *Luke14:26 (NKJV) "If anyone comes to Me and does not hate his father and mother, wife and children, brothers and sisters, yes, and his own life also, he cannot be My disciple".*

This scripture truly sums it all up. While it uses the word "hate", Jesus does not expect anyone to hate their family in the negative connotation of the word. What is meant is that your love for God through Jesus Christ should be so strong and prominent, that in comparison to your feelings about your family, it would almost seem that you hate them. It is a very stern way of saying that you should place far more regard and consideration to the service of Jesus Christ than you do with your family unless you are in fellowship with them in worship to God. To understand this reveals just how much emphasis God places on your life. How He proves that He wants the best for your life and how the best life you can have, is one that is surrendered to Him. He doesn't want to be in contention with you for your life, but instead wants to live harmoniously with you as He guides you through life. He wants to help you navigate the tough patches that you often find yourself in. He wants to help you overcome hurdles that block your path, to prevent you from advancing to the next best thing in your life. Most of all, He wants to be right there with you as a shoulder to cry on when you're met disappointment from one of the family members or friends who has let you down.

The third and final false god I want to make you aware of, is one that might surprise you. This false or idol god is yourself. Typically, when you make yourself an idol god, you don't believe in the true and living God. This could be for one or two reasons. It could be due to another religion that you worship. There are several religions deny the existence of a true God. Their doctrine does not support the idea of a Theocratic or God-ruled world. Instead, the teach that each person or individual is his own god. They teach that no one or no thing should govern how you live your life. You should be in control of your own life and determine your own rules for how you live.

The other reason you make yourself a god, is not because you have chosen any religion or cult, but simply because you just want to live your way. No religion taught you, but you just taught yourself that you should be able to be like Burger King and have everything your way. This actually may work for you for a while, but eventually everything in your life will start to crumble and fall apart. You cannot live in a world that God created and think you can make it your own. Everything in the world that you take part in or associate with, is the workmanship of God's hands. When He starts to separate you from it all, you can no longer survive. You were not meant to be alone and without resources. God has a way of stripping you down until you have nothing left. Just like He did to Job in the bible. Job lost everything until he surrendered to God and acknowledged that he was not equal to or greater than God. As a matter of fact, Job admitted that it was only because of God that he lived through the loss of everything else except his life. Remember, earlier I told you that in Exodus 20, it states that God is a jealous God and will not allow you to have any other gods before him… including yourself.

Much of self-worship is driven by vanity. It is possible to get so full of yourself because of how you look or how you want to appear to others. Vanity will draw you away from God and cause you to be self-centered. Be very careful of vanity in your life. It was for this very reason that Lucifer the angel was kicked out of heaven and down into the earth realm. He was a magnificent, created angel who was full of wisdom and perfect in beauty. The problem came in when he started thinking too much of himself and focusing on his beauty and attributes more than he did the God who created him that way. For this reason, he lost his position in heaven as was kicked out. If you are not careful you too can fall into this demise.

Because we live in the social media age, vanity is more prevalent now than ever before. Most people use social media to search out others to covet their lifestyles. Celebrities are a prime target. Obviously, they have millions of dollars, and they spend them on fancy houses, cars, clothes, and jewelry. Unfortunately, if you are vain, you seek out the lifestyles of these celebrities and try to live like them. Moreover, you then post the pictures of yourself on social media for all your friends and family to see you. You then, like Lucifer, let the compliments go to your head and you get deeper and deeper in vanity. The more compliments you get, the more you want and seek after. Before you know it, you're spending hours and hours on the internet and social media, to the point that you no longer have time for God. Or worse, you have no interest in God because you are only interested in yourself. Falling into this life of self-centeredness puts you in contention with God. You are fighting with Him for your attention. He wants you to worship him, which you were created for, but you are consumed with worshiping yourself.

You must remember that Jesus is King of kings, and Lord of lords. He is above all and over all things. In His kingdom, there is but one king. He is Christ the King. He created you to worship Him. He will never worship you, nor will He ever allow you to worship another beside Him. Regardless of whether you worship money, your family, or yourself, you are fighting with God by choosing idol gods. God knows that your best life is lived with Him and He is constantly trying to have that relationship with you. However, you continue to fight Him for your best life, because you choose to put everything else before Him. The beauty of it is that God will never stop fighting for a harmonious and reciprocal relationship with you, even if He must fight with you to get it.

### Personal Testimonial

I have to say that I am guilty of worshiping two out of three of these false gods at some point in my life. I think ninety-five percent of all who read this will say they've had money problems to the point of worshiping it. For whatever reason, there is always the thought that you can never get enough money. It seems just when you think you have enough, something comes up that requires you to spend a large portion of what you have or you see something you really want and you splurge on purchasing it. You can even just have poor money management skills like I did. I was raised with the philosophy that "you can't take it with you". With this mindset it meant that whenever you get money, you should spend it on whatever you want because you can't take it with you with you die. While it is very true that you cannot take money with you when you die, I had to also realize that I need to utilize it to provide for myself and my future while I was alive.

Much of my life was lived like this. It wasn't until my late twenties, that I began to take money more seriously. I took financial courses that helped me get myself on track financially. One was offered at our church, and it was "The Crown Financial Ministry" financial course. The other was a course by Dave Ramsey, the world renowned biblical financial coach. From these two courses I learned the principles of managing money through giving, paying, saving, and investing. All were in God's plan for pleasing Him, which created increase in my finances because of God's blessing being upon them.

The other false idol I had was myself. There was a period in my life when I only cared about me. I had a knowledge of God, but I did not worship Him. I only was interested in what pleased me and made me feel good. I was even vain and let the compliments of others go to my head. There were several females who often compliment me on how attractive I was. There were even men along with women who complimented how I dressed and the clothes I wore. I let this become the focus of my life and I didn't give God the proper attention because I was containing it all for myself. At the time, I didn't realize I had made myself to be an idol God, but when my life started to fall apart, I realized it quickly. Thankfully I came to my senses and surrendered my life to God and devoted myself to serving Him. He has only made me stronger, wiser, and better over the years and I am eternally grateful for it.

## The Challenge

1. Examine your life to see if you are a victim of idolatry?

2. Could there possible be people or things in your life that you worship and didn't realize before now?

3. Are you aware of your false god(s) but just don't know how to overcome them?

4.  Are you self-centered and are more into yourself than you are in God?

5.  How much time to you spend on the social media vs reading your bible or praying?

6.  Whatever is hindering a healthy relationship between you and God, start to wean yourself away from it, and start spending more time with God.

# CHAPTER NINE

.........................................................................................................

# SURRENDER

It goes without saying that the most proficient way to live your life is through a healthy relationship with God. It sounds cliché and taboo in this day and time, but in the same manner it is highly critical. Whether you want to acknowledge it or not, the world has changed. While everything seems so much better now, you would think that you need God less than you used to. Sure, as it relates to being successful and having wealth, this is the perfect time for it to happen. There are far more opportunities to gain wealth and popularity now, than ever before. There are even children who are under the age of thirteen, who own their own multi-million-dollar businesses. Technology and social media have made networking so easy that virtually everyone can do it. The more people you can reach, obviously, the more successful you can be. With all this great reward, there is less credit given to God. Without regard for God, then you are turned over to your own devices and means, which is dangerous. The more you get, the more you want, and you will do whatever you can to get it. So, on the contrary, we need God more today than we ever did. Simply because there are so many distractions working against Him than ever before. You need Him to help you gain the prosperity you desire in life, and to give you the wisdom to help you manage it without losing your soul.

This world that we live in has flipped upside down, metaphorically speaking. Everything that we were raised to think was wrong is now right and everything we were raised to think was right is now wrong. This comes as no surprise, because the world is ever changing, and people and things are evolving. However, to maintain balance in your life and not lose yourself amongst all these changes, you must cling to the only one who is and always has been the same.

> *Malachi 3:6 (NKJV) "For I am the Lord, I do not change. Therefor you are not consumed, O sons of Jacob".*

God declares unto you that you are His son or daughter through covenant relationship. He has never changed and will never change. He shall forever be the Alpha and Omega. He shall forever be All-wise, All-knowing, and All-powerful. His desire is to protect you from all things unholy and all things of this world that bring confusion to you. He desires for you to surrender to Him so that He can be your firm foundation for life. God understands that it is necessary for you to live in this world, but He does not want you to be consumed by the ways of this world.

> *Romans 12:1-2 (NKJV) "I beseech you therefore, brethren, by the mercies of God, that you present your bodies a living sacrifice, holy acceptable to God, which is your reasonable service. And do not be conformed to this world, but be transformed by the renewing of your mind, that you may prove what is that good and acceptable, and perfect will of God".*

The Apostle Paul said it best here in this scripture he wrote to the Roman citizens. He urged them to surrender themselves fully unto God in a manner that was similar to what Jesus Christ did on the cross. Jesus became a sacrifice who actually died for us. Paul only asked that you be a living sacrifice. Meaning you don't have to die physically, certainly not by crucifixion on a cross, but that you spiritually, mentally, emotionally, and physically surrender and submit yourself to God as a living sacrifice. His desire is for you to be transformed by renewing your mind and not being consumed and conformed to the ways of this world. God wants you to maintain a dedication unto Him and honor His will and His way. He ends the verse by saying that choosing to surrender to God is your reasonable service, or the least you can do for a savior who literally died so that you could have the best of life.

Surrendering your life to God is not a burden as some would have you to think. There has been a stigma on Christianity or living by faith to where you would think that it is almost like serving a prison sentence. So many people think you can not enjoy life as a Christian because you are too limited in what you can do. This is not the case at all. As a Christian, you can still enjoy parties or social gatherings. You can still date and have a courtship with who you're attracted to. Life is still the same normal as you've always thought. There is one difference, however, and that is boundaries and honor unto God. As you live and enjoy life, God does expect that you will use caution and restraint in your actions and activities. As a matter of fact, one of the fruit of the spirit spoken of in the book of Galatians chapter five is self-control. Exercising self-control in your life is as much for your benefit as it is for God. Let's face it, you do this anyway probably every day. When you're driving, if the speed limit is fifty-five, you likely restrain from any urge to go above that limit. The reason is because you think of your safety and possibly getting a speeding ticket. This respect that you show to the legal system and your own safety, is the same respect that you should show to God. Consequently, when you show respect to the legal system, you are also honoring God, if you are surrendered to Him. As much as he requires you to honor Him spiritually, He also expects you to honor the law of the land.

To be surrendered to God means we must look at life with a reverse perspective. Instead of doing things to respect others and honor them, we should do those same things to those same people to honor God, and the people are honored by default. This means you do the same good things, but your motive is not to please people but to please God.

> *Proverbs 16:7-9 (NKJV) "When a man's ways please the Lord, He makes even his enemies to be at peace with him. Better is a little with righteousness, than vast revenues without justice. A man's heart plans his way, but the Lord directs his steps".*

The wisdom of Solomon transcends time and is worth as much now as when he wrote it thousands of years ago. He makes it very clear in this scripture that the objective in life is to please God. But God never requires you to do anything for Him and there is not a reward associated with it. Obviously, you should never get into a bargaining game with God to do tit-for-tat, but when you honor God because you love and worship Him, there is always a reward. One of the greatest rewards here is peace with your enemies. God doesn't always destroy your enemies, as you might want Him to, but this scripture tells you that He will make them be at peace with you. One of the best benefits of a life surrendered to God is peace. Peace with your enemies. Peace with your family. Peace with your problems. Peace with all the things you don't understand in life. God is Peace and peace is beautiful. To life a life that is without stress and worry because you are at peace is priceless.

As the scripture continues, it is better to have peace with righteousness, than to have a wealth of everything you want in life without justice and peace with God. It is better to live in harmony with God than it is to live in contention with Him while seeking have your own way. All you have to do is set your heart to surrender to God as the last part of the verse says. You must plan to establish your life with God, then He will direct your steps. He will guide you every step of the way in your life. He will minister to you His word, which will illuminate your steps and path. He will speak to you and advise you on your actions. He will feed your soul with wisdom, knowledge, and understanding. But most of all, He will hold you and comfort you. He will sooth your pain and wipe the tears from your eyes when the pressure of life gets tough. He will confirm His love for you every day. You will never again feel lonely.

> *Psalm 23:1-6 (NKJV) "The Lord is my shepherd; I shall not want. He makes me to lie down in green pastures; He leads me beside the still waters. He restores my soul; He leads me in paths of righteousness for His name's sake. Yea though I walk through the valley of the shadow of death, I will fear no evil; for You are with me; Your rod and Your staff, they comfort me. You prepare a table before me in the presence of my enemies; You anoint my head with oil; My cup runs over. Surely goodness and mercy shall follow me all the days of my life and I will dwell in the house of the Lord forever".*

This scripture from David says a whole lot and you have probably heard it or even recited it before at some point in your life. But the problem with most people is that they memorize the verses to the point that they can recite them, but unfortunately, they don't get the full understanding of what is being said. But of course, that's the case with some people with all scripture. But that's for another time. Nevertheless, with this one, David is referencing himself to God as David's sheep are to him.

When you devote your life to God, you become like sheep are to a shepherd. God is the ultimate shepherd. With Him you never want for anything. With Him. God provides you with food and water that you can peacefully enjoy as sheep do in green pastures beside water brooks. When you become weary with the cares of life, God restores comfort to your soul. As it relates to righteous living in this cruel and sinful world, you won't have to try to maintain spiritual integrity all by yourself. God is right there to lead you. To provide you with strength within so that you can overcome the desires to do wrong and instead lean toward righteousness in thoughts, words, and actions. He is not doing this just for your well-being, but He also has to protect the integrity of His name. He must guarantee that everyone who sees or interacts with you can see influence of God on your life. As others see the blessed life that you live through Jesus Christ, it will cause them to want a relationship with Him as well. Finally, the scripture states that God will take away fear from your life. Even if the tragedy of death is towering over you, you can face the situation and have no fear. This can only be accomplished with the faith of knowing that God is with you. You find comfort in His ability to ward off evil and destruction with His staff, while at the same time, keeping you in the herd with His rod. Note that the rod is not for punishment, only discipline and guidance. The greatest promise of all is that goodness and mercy will be never-ending staples in your life, and ever shall you be in the presence of the Lord.

Your life is best lived when you are surrendered to God. There are countless promises, from unconditional love, to grace and mercy, to the fruit of the Spirit. If you are already surrendered to God, then you fully understand everything you have read. You are rejoicing and bearing witness in agreement to the scriptures. However, if you are not surrendered to God for any or all the reasons described in this book, then you must make the decision right now. Don't wait, make the decision now to surrender your life to God. Just pray a simple prayer confessing all your sins and faults and ask God to forgive you of them and give you the strength to change your heart and mind so you will never go back to those things again. Just know that God loves you and doesn't want to fight with you. But you are in control of the fight. As long as you fight against Him, God will continue to fight against you. He will never stop fighting until He has all of you. Wave your white flag in surrender, throw in the towel and let God have control of your life. I guarantee you will not regret it. Instead, you will live a fulfilled life with purpose that brings joy with each new day.

```
_____
    Personal Testimonial
_____
_____
_____
_____
```

I am so glad that I took the step of faith to completely surrender my life to God. However, I must tell you that it wasn't easy. I was just like you probably are scared and afraid, not feeling worthy and doubtful of living up to the expectations. This is exactly how I was. I knew that I needed God and for the most part, wanted God. I was just not sure he wanted me. I wondered why God would want to be a part of my life. I based my inhibitions on my actions. For I lived in sin and did things that were wrong like we all have. I lied, fornicated, gambled, hated people. I even thought I was better than others. For people that I thought did worse things than I did, I deemed them to be stupid. I didn't realize that what they did was no worse than what I was doing, but because I was blinded by unrighteousness, I couldn't see my own sins, only the sins of others. With the terrible actions I carried out every day, I didn't think God wanted anything to do with me. However, because I needed Him so badly, I began to seek out the possibility of connecting with Him. As I learned about God, I realized that God does not judge me as much on what I do as He does on who I am. This is probably the greatest revelation I have ever gained from God. You see, when God created me, He made me in His image and likeness. He made me to a son of His. That is who I am. Sure, because I live in a human flesh, I will never be perfect physically and I will make mistakes as long as I live. God can forgive me of those mistakes and get me back on the right track. However, if I ever deny who I am, then God can never forgive me. Because if I deny who I am as a son of God, then I deny who He is as God. This is an unforgivable act that you can not recover from.

So learning about God, helped me realize that God does not expect me to be perfect, just His son. With this, I surrendered to God and made Jesus Lord of my life. It was the best decision I ever made in my life. The Spirit of God dwells deeply within me and I am abounding in love, joy, peace, goodness, meekness, gentleness, self-control, faith, and tolerance. These are the fruit of the Spirit or the essence of a person who has surrendered to a life with God through Jesus Christ.

The Challenge

1. Have you surrendered your life to God?

2. If not, what is hindering you from doing so?

3. Are you consumed with or distracted by the things of the world that prevents you from surrendering?

4. Will you give yourself over to God today?

5. Wave the white flag of surrender and let God have control of your life.